Pre–School Success Plan

An Independent Play Provider's Guide to

Working with Toddlers

by P A Sampson

Pre-School Success Plan:
An Independent Play Providers Guide to Working with Toddlers.
by P A Sampson

Published by PAS Publishing
www.paspublishing.co.uk

Ebook ISBN: 978-1-9999110-0-3

Contents

Introduction:

Why Work with Pre-Schoolers?

The Benefits of Working with Young Children

There is nothing quite like working with pre-school children, and teachers, carers and play facilitators give many different reasons why they are happy that they made that career choice:

Young children are often described as 'sponges' due to their incredible ability to soak up new information; combined with their openness to learning, this makes teaching pre-schoolers one of the most rewarding occupations.

Children's lives are geared around having fun, and this freedom from adult concerns and anxieties helps those who teach them to 'lighten up,' put their own problems into perspective and rekindle the spirit of joy that is the birthright of every child.

Children are also infinitely creative and adventurous, constantly exploring their new environments and increasingly mastering new skills. Watching this process helps adults to appreciate their own world with fresh eyes and become more engaged, patient and compassionate people. Then there are the career opportunities. Pre-schoolers make up a large segment of the market and there is always a demand to find new, exciting ways to entertain and educate them.

Helping the Next Generation

Working with pre-school children provides teachers and activity providers with a way to make a difference in the lives of others, and to bring a sense of meaning to their own lives. Some even feel 'called' to this career, seeing it as a vocation, while others grow into their role as they watch their students grow and develop.

Providing high quality activities for children at the pivotal pre-school age benefits them physically, academically and psychosocially, preparing them for the challenge of the school environment and helping to provide a strong foundation for their positive development.

Physically, high quality pre-school activities can help children to improve:

- Balance
- Co-ordination
- Gross and/or fine motor skills

Providing children with these skills at this influential age will stand them in good stead for participation in sports, P.E. and other physical activities in school. This makes it more likely that children will enjoy these activities and make good progress.

Academically, pre-school activities should:

- Enhance listening and response skills.
- Promote language skills (e.g. through storytelling).
- Instil an appreciation of music and the arts.

By stimulating cognitive development, children will start school already equipped with valuable skills.

Psychosocially, pre-school activities should:

- Introduce children to positive role models outside of their family circle.
- Provide a warm and nurturing environment.
- Promote positive peer interactions and build rewarding relationships.

For many pre-school children, group activity sessions will be the first time their actions have been led by an adult who is not a member of their family unit. It is vital that a teacher or play programme provider conducts themselves as an excellent role model, balancing professionalism with warmth and friendliness. By appealing to both parents and children, such pre-school teachers will build a reputation which places them ahead of less suitable competitors.

Toddlers will also be forging early peer relationships at this time and learning valuable lessons regarding sharing, communication and supporting one another. A good play leader will reinforce positive behaviour while skilfully managing challenging situations.

First Steps:
Finding a Venue

What's Available

Whether you are offering music therapy, dance classes or art and craft sessions, there are plenty of avenues to go down to secure that first venue. Some (usually experienced) pre-school instructors hire or even buy their own premises and focus on attracting customers through effective marketing, while others prefer to work within an existing provision, adding their specific classes or courses to what is already on the activities timetable.

If you are interested in going down the latter route, you will need to research your target area in some depth to find out what venues are out there and what they currently offer parents of pre-school children. Pay particular attention to those organisations advertising for 'freelance' instructors or play workers or for employees to run 'casual' or 'flexible' activities. This indicates that the organisers may be open to providing space for an independent facilitator running their own programme.

To reach out to a prospective venue and arrange a preliminary meeting, facilitators can send emails, write formal letters or call the venue directly.

Pre-school activity providers in your area might include:

- Nurseries and Pre-schools
- Day Centres
- Performing Arts Schools
- Holiday Resorts
- Leisure Centres
- Church Groups
- Cruise Ships
- Children's Centres
- Special Schools
- Mobile Play Buses
- Libraries

Before meeting with a potential venue manager, read up about them via their website and any literature you find, paying particular attention to their vision, aims, objectives and charter.

Example:
Appealing to Sure Start Children's Centres

Securing space at a Sure Start Children's Centre can be demanding. To fulfil their remit as a 'Sure Start' Children's Centre, each centre must offer high quality, affordable activities for parents and children. Facilitators who are looking to work in this environment will need to convince the managers—and sometimes a parental advisory board—that their sessions will add value to the centre's activity calendar. Even privately run Sure Start centres will have a contract and a Service Level Agreement (SLA) with the Local Authority (LA), which puts pressure on them to deliver a great service.

For those who have never taught in a pre-school setting before, it is worth considering applying for an assistant facilitator role to gather some valuable work experience before taking the plunge. This can also be a good way to network and find out about openings in other areas.

Once you do secure yourself a venue, and before you run your first session, be sure to familiarise yourself will all of their policies and procedures, in particular their fire, Health & Safety and safeguarding policies.

Going it Alone

Another route to consider is to run your own club by renting (or even buying) studio space. This may suit you if you value your autonomy and are confident you can master the variety of skills needed to turn your club into a success (see pp 14-23 for a breakdown of these). For example, you will quickly need to assess your target market and create a workable strategy for attracting parents and children to your door.

Again, you might find work experience as a play assistant invaluable before biting the bullet and stepping out on your own two feet. And though you won't need any kind of qualification to run freelance activity sessions, it won't harm your cause to pick up one of the many awards, certificates, diplomas or foundation degrees on offer (e.g. Certificate of Playwork). These can also open doors to getting a future degree in Child Development or similar fields.

Alternatively, you might think about taking on a franchise or becoming a certified provider of activities via a 'Learn through Play' organisation (e.g. Hip Hop Tots®). This will give you a head start in terms of branding and lesson planning, and you may also receive support with marketing materials and stationery.

As well as covering the rent or mortgage on your activity venue, you will need to find the funds for:

- Equipment

- Materials

- Refreshments

- Buildings/contents Insurance

- PLI (Public Liability Insurance)

- Professional Indemnity Insurance

- Music Licences (PLR, PRS)

- DBS (formerly CRB) checks

- Stationery

- Marketing Materials

In short, running your own pre-school activity sessions is very demanding, and if you are not 100% certain you can handle the pressure, it is advisable to start out by securing space at an existing facility. This will enable you to build up a reputation before you consider going it alone.

Parties and 'One Off' Events

Children's parties and charity or community events can often be an ideal way to create a buzz around your activity programme, giving people the chance to sample a session before deciding whether they want to commit to regular sessions.

Children's parties in particular are becoming increasingly popular ways for activity providers of all kinds: art, crafts, dance, music, etc., to bump up their earnings while reaching out to a wider audience.

Children's parties tend to last from between two to three hours, and an example format might be:

- 10m   Welcome children, collect food choices.
- 1-1.5h   Activity session.
- 30m   Food and cake.
- 20-45m   Games/general play.
- 10m   Party bags and pick-up.

There should be a healthy stock of membership forms available, for those parents who want to book their pre-school child a place there and then, as well as party-bag sized flyers/leaflets.

Activities provided at charity fundraisers and community events (festivals, carnivals, shows, etc.) are usually free, taster activities which can be treated as a marketing expense and, occasionally, a chance for some good quality PR (particularly if the event is covered by the press). Choosing the right event is crucial, since targeting the wrong market will have little if any benefit no matter how big the turnout. On the other hand, even a modest village fayre can make a huge difference if those attending are of the right demographic and the local newspaper or radio station happen to be in attendance.

To make the most of the expense of running a free session, it is important that there is a clear and simple way for interested parents to sign their children up for a session or term of activities.

At the very least there should be a supply of leaflets to pick up or for handing out on the day. However, the IT literate activity provider should also ensure that their website/social media profile is up and running and clearly displayed. QR codes are free to create and enable parents with mobile phones to instantly connect with the provider's website without having to pick up any bits of paper.

Another option, which is often used to stir up interest in a new activity, is to set up a one-off free workshop and combine this with refreshments and even a free giveaway (e.g. a T-shirt or children's bracelet).

How Toddlers Learn

Children's Bodies; Children's Minds

During their pre-school years, children grow and develop amazingly quickly—both physically and psychologically—and the abilities of a five-year-old are vastly superior to those of a two-year-old, presenting a challenge to the pre-school playworker.

Psychologically, the number of nerve cells (neurons) in the child's brain continues to increase until around the age of two, after which the brain appears to 'prune' these connections. The reasons for this are not fully understood, but it is likely to be due to increasing specialisation of the brain into distinct areas.

The prefrontal cortex seems to be particularly important at this stage, and is involved in picking up and mastering new skills, so it is important that the child's environment is rich and stimulating—in the right way—so that useful connections are forged from the beginning. This area of the brain also directs attention, so pre-school is the perfect time to teach general learning skills such as listening and responding (as in following instructions) and concentration. As toddlers are still mastering this so-called 'executive function' of the brain, facilitators will need to keep instructions simple, repeat activities often and organise sessions so as to minimise distractions.

Commands also need to be given in plain language using as few words as possible.

Although pre-school children understand many more words than they can produce, their vocabulary and grammar are still very limited compared to those of adults.

Physically, the pre-school years see children developing significantly in terms of their balance, bodily awareness, strength, stamina, co-ordination and speed. Before the age of two, infants are still mastering the art of swaying to music, picking up items from the floor while standing and moving their whole arm to draw. Older pre-schoolers, on the other hand, will be able to run and jump, build towers from blocks and use their thumb and finger to hold pencils.

Content That Connects

From the above section, it should become clear that teaching pre-school children requires careful consideration in terms of the type of content provided and how the play space is organised.

When designing your lesson/activity plans and choosing the resources you will be using, the following guidelines should help:

- **Make it Simple**

Due to their developing comprehension of language (both vocabulary and grammar), any instructions need to be presented in plain language, using as few words as possible. Wherever possible, a sequence of instructions should be broken down into individual steps. For example, instead of asking a toddler to, 'fetch a pencil from the cardboard box, pick up a sheet of A4 and sit down at the table,' it would be better to split this into three steps:

1) Take a pencil from the brown box.

2) Pick up some paper.

3) Sit down by the table.

Pre-school children also benefit from plenty of repetition to help them remember instructions and to train their muscle memory.

- **Be Engaging**

Anyone who has spent time with pre-school children will tell you that the physical and social environment is an endless source of distraction; teachers and playworkers need to manage this by keeping the play environment organised and providing plenty of varied, engaging content. Research shows that the more stimulating a task is, the more time a child will spend paying attention to it and the less distractable they will be. This in turn helps them to develop a longer attention span overall which will assist them in becoming better learners. Pre-schoolers are keen to use all of their developing senses, so teachers need to think in terms of sound, texture, scent and taste as well as the more obvious visual stimulation through pattern and colour. Lively music, songs with actions and plenty of movement will all enhance learning as well as livening up your classes.

- **Be Adaptable**

One of the key skills for pre-school teachers and play facilitators to master is assessing the ability level of the children in their classes and pitching content at the right level. This is challenging due to both the fast pace of development and individual differences in that rate of growth. Experienced teachers and playworkers will create activities that can be easily simplified or made more demanding by the subtraction or addition of material or stages. For example, a dance/movement routine could be made up of a basic 'core' with additional layers of complexity added as necessary to meet the development level of the class.

- **Prioritise Safety**

Pre-school children are keen explorers and adventurers and this can get them into trouble at times! The first duty of a lesson provider is to provide a safe environment for their children. Obvious sources of danger are entrances and exits; falling and tripping hazards; sharp objects and toxic substances.

For free access to pre-school teaching resources and to generate your own ideas, visit SparkleBox (see **Resources** section).

Strength Through Support

Just as the first few months of an infant's existence are about weaning them from physical dependence on their primary caregiver, gradually empowering them to walk, talk and eat for themselves, the pre-school years see children enter the wider social world and moving from home-based to school-based learning.

Depending on how this transition is managed, children can emerge feeling secure and full of self-confidence, or anxious and lacking in self-belief (or, more commonly, a mixture of the two).

Although the foundation of their social development is built at home, the pre-school environment has a significant impact too, particularly since this is where new adults and children come into the picture.

Many toddler activity sessions, particularly in the early years, require parents to be involved, and it is important to ensure that children enjoy a positive experience of other adults as they begin to form so-called 'secondary attachments.' Therefore, pre-school teachers and playworkers should always be friendly, encouraging and approachable.

Pre-schoolers are also learning to co-exist with their peers and, for some, the need to share and consider the needs of others is a complete shock to the system. Pre-school teachers and playworkers need to be aware of this challenge and to work with parents and guardians to teach and demonstrate correct behaviour and to ensure that all children are treated fairly and given the chance to express themselves. Setting some house rules at the beginning of each programme, and reinforcing them during each session, will help to prepare pre-schoolers for the more disciplined environment of their school years.

Preparing for School

Every year, schools have the huge task of bringing in a new cohort of children, all at various stages of development and all with different home and experiential backgrounds, and turning them into successful students.

The issue of 'readiness'—how prepared reception year children are for the rigours of school—is a hot potato in education at the moment, with the NUT sometimes very scathing in their criticism of children's centres and nurseries for providing a poor range of low quality activities.

This gives switched-on freelance pre-school play facilitators a big opportunity to get ahead of competitors and target their sales pitches at the right level. By providing toddlers with activity programmes that enhance their physical, academic and social 'readiness,' these activity leaders will be a breath of fresh air to facility managers looking to prove themselves to school heads, LAs and other stakeholders. As mentioned earlier, privately run 'Sure Start' Children's Centres are particularly keen to provide high quality, value for money activities to ensure that their contract with the LA will be renewed. It is recommended that freelance play instructors codify this concept of readiness into a written policy that they can then hand out and discuss at meetings.

Familiarisation with the national curriculum, particularly Key Stage 1 (which applies to five to seven year-olds) can benefit pre-school arts instructors as they can more easily match their programmes' aims and objectives to the broad areas covered in school. A link to the latest national curriculum information is included in the **Resources** chapter.

Skills & Attributes Part 1:

The Core Skills

Are you Really Ready?

Regardless of how far you might be along your own path to teaching pre-school age children, now is a good time to take a deep breath and think hard about whether you are really ready to take the plunge and begin offering your services. While the only real test of your capabilities will come on the playroom floor itself, you need to go into this career with your eyes open and an honest appreciation of your strengths and weaknesses:

Here are some self-assessment questions you might want to ask yourself:

- What is it about working with pre-school children that inspires you (the **Introduction** mentions some of the reasons other playworkers have given)?
- Do you find it easy to engage with children? What will you do to make that positive connection?

- Do you already have experience of working with toddlers? If so, how will you use that to enrich your programme?

- If you don't have much experience, will you consider work experience, volunteering or a casual job first*?

- How do you plan to deal with challenging behaviour?

- Do you tend to get on well with other children's parents? How will you create a good impression on them?

- Of the skills listed below, which are your strengths and which need developing?

- How will you compensate for weak areas? Can you leverage family or friends, or will you need to outsource work (e.g. admin or IT)?

*There are many seasonal or casual roles which will help inexperienced play instructors or teachers to become familiar with the pre-school environment. Relevant jobs might include nursery or pre-school assistants, junior playworkers, activity co-ordinators or even Key Stage 1 Learning Support Assistants (LSAs). Sites such as Indeed or Monster will list vacancies. Alternatively, volunteering for organisations such as Sure Start, or taking on a work experience placement, can all help to build experience and make contacts.

Essential Skills for Teaching Pre-Schoolers

There are many useful skills to help with teaching a room full of toddlers, but we have selected eight 'core skills' that every pre-school teacher and playworker should have: class management, communication, creativity, enthusiasm, Health & Safety awareness, organisational ability, patience and a love of teaching children!

1. **Class Management**

Pre-school teachers and facilitators need to strike that delicate balance between being kind and friendly and being fair and in control. Children should not be afraid of you, so you must be warm and approachable, but you also have to set boundaries and be willing and able to reign in naughty behaviour.

2. **Communication**

Pre-school teachers have to be able to communicate well, both with children and their parents. Important information (e.g. Health & Safety guidelines) need to be presented clearly and regularly reinforced.

3. **Creativity**

Keeping children (and their parents) interested and engaged is a test of a playworker's imagination. Content should be kept fresh and, where possible, have an educational element to it. For example, in one session you might want to have children writing letters in the sand, while in another they might be singing rhymes.

4. **Enthusiasm**

Pre-school children respond well to energy, movement and a sense of fun. Being enthusiastic at all times—even on a rainy winter's morning—is the hallmark of a great teacher or activity instructor.

5. Health & Safety Awareness

Here is where you have a clear advantage if you are a parent or older sibling, or have plenty of experience working with children. As well as protecting toddlers from obvious sources of danger (sharp objects, big drops, hot drinks, etc.), teachers and facilitators need to be vigilant for more subtle hazards (e.g. toys that trap fingers, toxic paints, trailing shoelaces, etc.). Young children have an uncanny ability to get themselves into trouble, so adults need to keep a close eye on what's going on at all times.

6. Organisational Ability

Pre-school teachers and facilitators need to be able to create order out of chaos, deciding on the aims and objectives of a programme or session and designing a workable sequence of activities to achieve those aims.

7. Patience

Children develop at different rates, and while some pre-schoolers will immediately pick up a task, another might struggle. Pre-school teachers/instructors need to be prepared to repeat instructions and demonstrate skills over and over again without becoming annoyed or angry.

8. Love of Teaching Children

Fundamental to all of the above essential skills is the love of working with children of pre-school age. This type of work is not something that can be entered into in a half-hearted way, so teachers need to be sure they are absolutely dedicated to their occupation before starting out.

If you have any doubts about whether you possess the core skills and attributes listed above, you would probably benefit from gaining some work experience before offering your own sessions. Casual and temporary roles (often advertised as play assistant or pre-school support staff positions) can be found on all of the main job sites (e.g. Monster, Gumtree, Indeed, etc.) or you could just ask an existing teacher/instructor to help out or sit in on their sessions. Voluntary positions may also be available (e.g. at Sure Start children's centres).

Skills & Attributes Part 2:

Additional Skills

The following list of skills and attributes are not essential for teaching a pre-school activity programme, but they will go a long way towards helping you succeed as a self-employed playworker and business owner.

Time Management

Few business skills have more of an impact on success than the ability to manage your time efficiently. After all, time is money and the more prudent you can be with both, the quicker your road to financial freedom will be. But time management can be hard to put into practice; with multiple important tasks competing for your attention, which do you attend to first? Some business owners recommend a tool known as the 'priority matrix,' a simple four box table which sorts items into high or low importance and high or low urgency. This model can be adapted to add more boxes if needed. In any case, those tasks that are urgent are tackled first, in order of importance, followed by those which are important but less urgent. Delegation is also a powerful way to manage your time effectively (for example, you could enlist the help of parents in handing out flyers at their child's pre-school).

Admin & Housekeeping

Administration and housekeeping are not always the most enjoyable aspects of running your own business, but learning and mastering these skills are necessary to create a professional opinion of your abilities.

Skills worth brushing up on include:

- Organisation and storage of files and data (both physical and digital).
- Communication via email, letter, telephone and social media.
- Accounting and invoicing.
- Compliance and legislation.
- Budgeting/Financial Planning.
- Drawing up a contract.

There are plenty of reasonably priced—and sometimes free—courses available in most towns and cities covering all of the above skills areas and more.

Business Planning

Contrary to what many people think, writing a business plan does not need to involve a huge amount of time and paper. Unless you are looking to secure funding, in which case you will need to create a formal document, a business plan only needs to clearly set out your aims and objectives, describe your operational strategies and detail your financial projections. There are plenty of books and courses available for writing both formal and informal business plans.

Embracing the IT Age

Information Technology (computing) is becoming increasingly important in all lines of work, and brushing up on your skills can save you a lot of time and money as well as opening up new avenues of exploration (e.g. social media marketing, video blogging, etc.).

Just some of the IT skills that are worth adding to your toolkit are:

- Using email (writing, attaching documents, including recipients, sending, reading, organising).
- Social media (using Facebook, Twitter, LinkedIn and other platforms for finding customers and building relationships with them).
- Content creation (blogging, copywriting, etc.).
- Website skills (designing, building, hosting, using Content Management Systems).
- Writing documents.
- Using spreadsheets.
- Handling databases.

A Note on Websites

Learning how to host and administrate your own website has the potential of saving you a lot of money and is not that difficult for someone who is generally IT literate. Content Management Systems such as Wordpress can enable anyone to easily customise designs and add their own content and photographs, while hosting packages are available for less than ten pounds a month.

Marketing

Marketing skills are critical for any self-employed worker, and it would be easy to fill another book on that subject alone. Marketing encompasses a wide range of associated skills, including:

Market Research

In order to promote a product or service to the people most likely to buy or use it, a business has to have a deep and up-to-date knowledge of their target market. Ongoing market research is also needed to enable a business owner to identify improvements they can make, or opportunities they can take to attract and retain custom.

Effective market research for pre-school activity providers will pick up on all of the latest trends and hot topics in the Early Years education market and assess current provision to see if these are catered for in the target area. When a gap has been identified, forward-thinking activity providers can develop their service to fill it.

Much basic information on the market can be obtained by simply keeping aware of the word on the street. What are other activity providers offering? Has a certain type of session suddenly sprung up in multiple settings? What are parents of toddlers getting excited about?

If you are already running pre-school activity sessions, you should consider designing and giving out regular questionnaires and surveys to parents. Use these to keep in touch with their preferences, assess your strengths and weaknesses and aid in planning the next stage of the development of your business.

Networking and Consultation

Networking is a powerful tool for generating business and creating fresh ideas for future development, so it is definitely one marketing skill you should work on. Good networking focuses on both quality (getting the best contacts to help your business to thrive) and quantity (casting your net wide to involve influential people from multiple industries).

To start identifying those individuals and organisations you should get involved with, make a list of all of the groups that have an interest in children's education and activity provision. To start you off, these might include:

- Play organisations
- Charities
- Children's Centres
- Disability Groups
- Activity Clubs
- Community Groups
- Sports Centres
- Dance Studios
- Nurseries/Preschools

- Parents

All of these stakeholders can offer a different perspective on what your service needs to provide, with some presenting you with challenges to overcome and others with creative suggestions. For example, a disability advocacy group will be interested in how you intend to cater for wheelchair access and how you will structure activities to enable children with physical disabilities to take part. On the other hand, a local dance studio might have picked up on a popular dance routine that has inspired their members (often from a music video or TV programme). This might inspire you to create your own mini version of the routine for your pre-schoolers which will soon have parents talking to their friends (the 'cute' factor goes a long way).

Once you have a list of potentially useful networking contacts, you will need to create a plan to engage with them. Your plan should include:

- How to make contact (e.g. direct mail, email, phone call).
- Who to contact (e.g. decision makers, influential names).
- What information to include about your service (how can you gain their attention and support?).
- How you will organise your contacts (e.g. spreadsheet, database, paper records).

Engaging in relevant local consultations and advisory boards is a great way to meet the movers and shakers in your industry and to gain an understanding of community challenges and your part in solving them.

Promotion

Once you have built up a clear picture of your target market you can start creating a promotion strategy to build up interest in your classes. How you do this will depend largely on whether you will be working through another play setting or from your own premises.

If you are working through a pre-school, nursery, children's centre or other service provider you will be at an advantage since they will be promoting your class anyway (although the quality of that promotion can vary greatly). If you are working from your own venue, you will have to take control of all of your promotional activities.

In either case, you should keep the following three points in mind when designing your strategy:

1. Who are your target market?

2. Where do they live?

3. When is the ideal time to promote?

For pre-school activity providers, remember that the target market is NOT pre-school children! It is their parents, since they are the ones who will be spending money for their child to take part. Having said that, you will want to demonstrate, through your promotions, that your sessions are toddler-friendly, and if their child is attracted by a brightly coloured poster with a cute cartoon face—perhaps displayed at ground level—then that will help your cause!

Promotion can include free or low-cost elements, such as word of mouth marketing and some kinds of PR (e.g. where the press pick up on what you're doing and decide to report on it), but in most cases you will have to pay to spread the word. You will soon find that there are hundreds of ways to spend money on advertising, so you will need to be careful not to be frivolous (particularly if you are on a tight budget).

Some avenues worth exploring are:

- Flyers and brochures.
- Newspaper and magazine advertisements.
- Billboard posters.
- Radio and TV ads.
- Online advertising.

The least expensive option tends to be online advertising—either through display ads (e.g. Google Adwords) or social media promotion (e.g. Facebook promoted posts, Twitter sponsored tweets, Pinterest promoted pins, etc.). On the other end of the scale are TV ads which are very expensive in terms of both content creation and paying for airtime.

However, your most important consideration is ROI (Return on Investment). The absolute cheapest option is rarely the best, particularly if you get no response whatsoever.

Building your Online Brand

Online branding deserves its own chapter because the power of the internet to shape image and reach customers is now firmly established. In fact, it may be true to say that having an online presence is necessary for a business just to survive, let alone thrive, in the 21st Century.

Technology changes so rapidly in today's world that the modern business owner has to keep in touch or risk being cast aside. If you don't know what SEO stands for or are unconcerned about the latest changes in Google's search algorithm then you might want to do some research and get up to speed.

At the time of writing, local search optimisation, mobile technology, social networking and reputation management were some major areas of interest for internet-savvy businesses, but be aware that tomorrow there might be something else you need to know about.

The Power of Local

As soon as a business starts to look at its online presence, it very quickly bumps into Google. Why? Quite simply, the vast majority of internet users make use of its search engine to find information, including what to buy and where to get it. That fact alone gives Google a huge amount of power and responsibility when it comes to directing its users to relevant sources of information—as well as an incredible amount of data.

Google's research has revealed that people want to find information about what is in their local area, and that they are increasingly using mobile devices to access that information. Those business owners who have previously focused on getting their websites to the top of the list in Google's general search listings are in danger of becoming invisible because of two important developments:

1. The prominence of Google's My Business directory on the search pages (they sit above the general search listings).

2. The shift from big screens (laptops and desktops) to smaller ones (tablets, phablets and smartphones).

My Business is Google's business directory which links in to the Google + social network and many other Google properties (Google Search, Google Maps, etc.). If you have not done so already, creating a Google account and a Google My Business account (both free) should be top of your list of online activities. Although there are advanced techniques for boosting your My Business listing (e.g. using special coding known as 'schema markup' to pack your listing with extra information), simply selecting the relevant categories and filling in all of your details will often be enough to lift your business above all of the Google search listings when people are searching for you locally.

The shift to mobile device usage also means that when people are in your area and using Google to search for businesses like yours, only Google My Business directory listings can fit on their screens without the need to scroll. Even if your website is top of Google's search list, this simple fact could render your business invisible. When building your website (or having it built for you), make sure that the design is 'responsive.' This simply means that your site will adapt to whatever screen it appears on. You might even want to investigate creating a mobile app for your business.

To improve your website's performance, both locally and in general, you need to generate plenty of relevant and interesting content, otherwise you are wasting an opportunity to promote your business and build your reputation as a leader in the field of pre-school activity provision.

Some examples of content you might want to consider posting online are:

- Videos
- Press Releases
- Reviews
- Social Media Posts (see next section)

All content should be original and interesting to attract useful links from other websites and increase the chance of your webpages being ranked well by Google.

A Social Strategy

Having a strong social media presence can really boost your business in today's competitive marketplace, but using social media as a marketing tool is quite different to using it as a way to keep in touch with your friends.

There are countless social media networks out there on the World Wide Web, but many will be a waste of time in terms of promoting your business. Three of the most widely used networks, from a business perspective, are Facebook, Twitter and LinkedIn.

To be effective on social media, you should think about what you can provide to the community rather than what you can get out of it. You will also need to actually 'be social' by sharing content provided by others, for example by retweeting useful tweets, commenting on articles and blogs and sharing inspirational Facebook posts and LinkedIn updates. If you regularly provide valuable information, insightful advice and links to relevant resources you will build your reputation as an industry expert. People will also be more likely to reciprocate your generosity by sharing your social media content.

If you do feel the need to self-promote, don't overdo it or you risk annoying other people and having exactly the opposite effect to what you are trying to achieve.

Some pre-school activities (dance, performing arts, etc.) are visual in nature and you may wish to explore social media such as Instagram or Pinterest to engage with your target market.

However, you must obtain explicit permission from parents if you are posting images of children online.

Reputation Marketing

Reputation Management is the process of controlling how an individual or brand is perceived by others. It was originally a market-focused element of Public Relations (PR), but has recently become tied up with online review sites (e.g. Yelp!, Trip Adviser, etc.), social media networks and discussion forums. For a business, so-called ORM (Online Reputation Management) involves monitoring the World Wide Web for mention of their brand, maximising the effect of positive feedback and reducing the impact of negative feedback.

There are many companies now offering ORM as a service, but some of these take part in unethical practices such as writing fake positive reviews or criticising competitors. Above board tactics include consistently responding to feedback of all kinds, encouraging satisfied customers to leave reviews and avoiding negative reviews by compensating for poor service. Online feedback can also be used to improve your service, much like in-house surveys and questionnaires.

One Final Word

As you should now appreciate, teaching pre-school children requires a lot of preparation and the development of numerous skills. On the other hand, the rewards are worth it, with successful playworkers able to spend their working days alongside the most amazing people on this planet—children—

and seeing them develop into the creative, capable and caring adults that this world desperately needs.

What occupation could be more worthy than that?

Resources

You may find the following organisations and resources useful:

Government Resources:

List of Sure Start Children's Centres:

https://www.gov.uk/find-sure-start-childrens-centre

DBS (formerly CRB) advice:

https://www.gov.uk/disclosure-barring-service-check

Department of Education: The school curriculum: -
www.education.gov.uk/schools/teachingandlearning/curriculum

Early Years Foundation Stage information:

https://www.gov.uk/early-years-foundation-stage

Useful Non-Government Organisations:

Early Years Development and Childcare Partnership:

www.eydcp.com

Foundation Years website:

http://www.foundationyears.org.uk

The Children's Trust:

www.thechildrenstrust.org.uk

National Council for Voluntary Organisations:

www.ncvo.org.uk

PRS for Music Foundation:

www.prsformusicfoundation.com

The Artists' Information Company (an):

www.a-n.co.uk

National Arts Councils:

Arts Council England:

www.artscouncil.org.uk

Arts Council of Wales (Cyngor Celfyddydau Cymru):
www.artswales.org.uk

Arts Council of Northern Ireland (Airts Cooncil o Norlin Airlan): www.artscouncil-ni.org

Creative Scotland (Alba Chruthachail):

www.creativescotland.com

Other Facilitators' Resources:

The Artists Newsletter:

www.artweb.com/Artists-Newsletter

Arts Development UK:

www.artsdevelopmentuk.org

Advertising Standards Authority (ASA):

www.asa.co.uk

Skills Active:

www.skillsactive.com

SparkleBox (Free Teaching Resources):

www.sparklebox.co.uk

UN Convention on the Rights of the Child

www.unicef.org.uk/UNICEFs-Work/UN-Convention

For information about **LEAs and other local authority bodies,** contact your local council or visit their website.

www.ingramcontent.com/pod-product-compliance
Lightning Source LLC
Chambersburg PA
CBHW032252210326
41520CB00048B/3721